Table Of Contents

Chapter 1: Understanding Sundown Towns

Definition and Historical Context

Sundown towns are communities that were historically defined by their exclusionary policies aimed at maintaining an all-white population. This exclusion was often enforced through a combination of discriminatory laws, social intimidation, and, at times, outright violence. The term "sundown town" derives from the practice of requiring Black individuals to leave the town by sundown. These towns often displayed signs at their borders warning that Black people were not welcome after dark, creating an atmosphere of fear and exclusion that had lasting effects on racial dynamics in America.

The historical context of sundown towns traces back to the post-Civil War era, particularly during the Jim Crow period. In the late 19th and early 20th centuries, as African Americans sought to escape the oppressive conditions of the South, many sought refuge in Northern and Midwestern states. However, white residents in certain communities felt threatened by the prospect of integration and implemented measures to ensure their neighborhoods remained predominantly white. This was often achieved through local ordinances, restrictive covenants, and violence, demonstrating the lengths to which communities would go to maintain racial homogeneity.

The characteristics of sundown towns included not only the expulsion of Black individuals but also a façade of tolerance during daylight hours. Black people could often work, shop, or pass through these towns during the day but were subject to harassment and violence if they remained after sunset. Such policies created a paradoxical environment where Black residents were temporarily allowed but ultimately unwelcome. This duality reflects broader societal tensions regarding race relations and the systemic efforts to marginalize African Americans even in spaces that appeared accessible.

The impact of sundown towns has reverberated into modern racial dynamics, shaping perceptions and interactions within communities. Many towns that were once sundown towns continue to grapple with their legacies, as descendants of both the original residents and those who were excluded confront the historical injustices that have persisted over generations. The patterns of segregation and racial profiling that emerged from these towns can still be observed today, influencing contemporary discussions about race, equity, and justice.

Understanding the legacy of sundown towns requires a commitment to documenting and preserving their histories. Efforts to educate communities about this past, including personal narratives from descendants of sundown town residents, are crucial in addressing the ongoing impacts of these exclusionary practices. By examining the sociological implications and legal frameworks surrounding sundown towns, society can better comprehend how these historical contexts continue to shape modern America and contribute to ongoing racial disparities.

Characteristics of Sundown Towns

Sundown towns are characterized by a distinct set of features that reflect their historical context and ongoing impact on American society. One notable characteristic is the permissiveness of daytime access for Black individuals. These towns often allowed Black people to enter during daylight hours, primarily to work, shop, or conduct business. However, this limited access was strictly controlled, with the implicit understanding that they were expected to leave before sunset. This temporal restriction created an environment of fear and exclusion, reinforcing the notion of racial superiority among the white residents while simultaneously marginalizing Black individuals.

Expulsion is another defining characteristic of sundown towns. Many communities utilized intimidation tactics, including threats and violence, to drive Black residents out of the area. This could manifest in various forms, from aggressive policing to mob violence, all aimed at maintaining racial homogeneity. The consequences for Black individuals who defied these unwritten rules were severe, often resulting in physical harm or even death. Such actions were not just random acts of racism but were part of a broader system of racial control that ensured the community remained predominantly white.

Enforcement mechanisms were crucial in sustaining the sundown town's racial policies. Local law enforcement often played an active role in upholding these discriminatory practices, whether through direct participation in acts of violence or by turning a blind eye to them. This complicity created a culture of impunity, where white residents felt emboldened to act on their prejudices without fear of legal repercussions. The police became enforcers of racial boundaries, ensuring that the social order remained intact according to the town's racial hierarchy.

The historical analysis of sundown towns reveals a pattern of systemic racism that has shaped not only the communities themselves but also the broader societal landscape. Understanding these historical contexts is essential for recognizing how the legacy of sundown towns continues to influence modern racial dynamics. The impact is evident in ongoing segregation, economic disparities, and social tensions that can be traced back to these towns' exclusionary practices. This historical lens allows us to comprehend the roots of contemporary issues related to race and community development.

Finally, the legacy of sundown towns persists in various forms today, influencing the narratives and experiences of descendants of those who lived in these communities. Personal stories and historical documentation serve as vital tools for understanding the profound effects of these towns on both individuals and communities. Educational programs that address the legacy of sundown towns can help foster awareness and promote dialogue about race relations in America, encouraging societies to confront their past and work towards a more inclusive future. By recognizing these characteristics, we can better understand the shadows that linger in contemporary society and the ongoing struggle for racial equity.

The Origin of the Term

The term "sundown town" emerged during the late 19th and early 20th centuries as a descriptor for communities in the United States that adopted policies and practices aimed at maintaining racial homogeneity. These towns were characterized by a strict unwritten rule that prohibited Black individuals from being present after sunset. The origin of the term can be traced back to the signs that were often posted at the town's borders, which warned that Black people had to leave by dusk. This practice reflected the broader systemic racism prevalent in American society, where segregation was enforced not only through laws but also through social norms and violence.

The concept of sundown towns gained traction during a time when Jim Crow laws were at their peak, codifying racial segregation in the Southern states and influencing attitudes in the North. Although the legal frameworks differed, many Northern towns adopted similar exclusionary practices. The term highlights the paradox of racial acceptance during daylight hours, where Black individuals could work, shop, and pass through, but were met with hostility and violence if they remained after dark. This duality illustrates the deep-seated racism that permeated both social interactions and community governance.

Historically, sundown towns employed various means to enforce racial exclusion. Local law enforcement often played a complicit role, either turning a blind eye to violence against Black individuals or actively participating in their expulsion. This enforcement was not limited to physical violence but also included economic intimidation, where Black workers could risk their livelihoods by attempting to remain in these towns after dark. The term "sundown" thus encapsulates a broader culture of fear and control that was designed to preserve racial purity in these communities.

In contemporary discussions about racial dynamics, the legacy of sundown towns remains relevant. The historical practices that led to the establishment of these towns have contributed to ongoing issues of segregation, economic disparity, and social stratification. Descendants of both residents and those expelled from these towns carry the weight of this history, and the term serves as a reminder of the long-lasting impacts of systemic racism. Understanding the origin and implications of the term "sundown town" is crucial for addressing the current racial tensions that persist in many American communities.

Efforts to document and preserve the histories of sundown towns are vital for educating future generations about this dark chapter in American history. Educational programs that explore the legacy of these towns can foster a deeper understanding of the societal structures that allowed such discrimination to flourish. By examining personal narratives, legal frameworks, and sociological impacts, communities can begin to confront the lingering effects of sundown towns and work towards healing and reconciliation. The term itself, while rooted in a painful past, can serve as a catalyst for dialogue and change in the pursuit of a more equitable society.

Chapter 2: Historical Analysis of Sundown

Towns in the United States

The Rise of Sundown Towns in America

The rise of sundown towns in America occurred primarily in the late 19th and early 20th centuries, reflecting the broader societal attitudes toward race during that time. These communities implemented various discriminatory practices designed to maintain racial homogeneity, often through informal agreements among residents, local ordinances, or even violence. The term "sundown town" itself signifies a clear and chilling message: Black individuals were expected to leave by sunset, highlighting the racial segregation that permeated American life. This practice was not merely a relic of the past but a systemic approach to uphold white supremacy in many regions of the United States.

Sundown towns often allowed Black individuals to enter during daylight hours for work or commerce but enforced strict measures to ensure their departure before nightfall. This duality underscored a paradox within these communities: while Black individuals could contribute economically, they were simultaneously dehumanized and viewed as a threat to the social order. The presence of signs stating "Nigger, Don't Let the Sun Set on You Here" served as a stark warning, reinforcing a culture of intimidation. Such overt racial hostility was complemented by subtler forms of exclusion, often manifesting in social ostracization and economic disenfranchisement.

The enforcement of sundown town policies was typically carried out by local law enforcement, community vigilantes, or even informal neighborhood groups. These enforcers wielded significant power, perpetuating a climate of fear that discouraged Black individuals from challenging the status quo. Instances of violence were not uncommon, as towns would rally to defend their racial boundaries.

This violent enforcement solidified the social fabric of these communities, allowing them to maintain their white-only status through terror and coercion. The legacy of this enforcement continues to shape discussions around race and policing in modern America.

Understanding the historical context of sundown towns is crucial for analyzing their lasting impact on contemporary racial dynamics. Many of these towns remain predominantly white, with the historical narratives surrounding their founding often ignored or sanitized. The social and economic consequences of this exclusionary practice are still felt today, as communities grapple with issues of systemic racism and inequality. The descendants of those who enforced or lived within sundown towns often find themselves navigating a complex legacy that intertwines pride in their community with the shame of its exclusionary past.

In recent years, there has been a growing movement to document and preserve the histories of sundown towns, emphasizing the need for education and awareness. Initiatives aimed at acknowledging this dark chapter in American history seek to confront the ongoing ramifications of such segregationist policies. By engaging in open discussions about the past, communities can begin to dismantle the barriers that persist in shaping racial relations today. As we move further into the future, it is essential to recognize the significance of sundown towns in understanding the broader narrative of race in America and to foster dialogues that promote healing and reconciliation.

Key Historical Events and Figures

The history of sundown towns in America is marked by a series of significant events and key figures who shaped the racial landscape of various communities. Beginning in the late 19th century and reaching into the mid-20th century, sundown towns were designed to create and maintain an all-white population through a combination of local ordinances, social practices, and outright violence. These towns often employed signs that warned Black individuals to leave by sundown, reinforcing a culture of exclusion and intimidation. The establishment of sundown towns reflects the broader context of systemic racism and segregation that permeated American society during this period.

One of the pivotal events in the rise of sundown towns was the Great Migration, when millions of African Americans moved from the rural South to urban centers in the North and West in search of better opportunities. As Black populations began to increase in certain areas, white residents often reacted with hostility, leading to the establishment of sundown policies to preserve the racial homogeneity of their towns. This backlash was often fueled by fear of economic competition and a desire to maintain social order as defined by white supremacy. The violent expulsion of Black residents from these towns became a chilling hallmark of this era.

Prominent figures also played crucial roles in both the perpetuation and the challenge of sundown town practices. Local leaders, including mayors and law enforcement officials, often turned a blind eye to the violence or actively participated in the enforcement of sundown policies. In contrast, civil rights activists emerged in various regions to combat the injustices faced by African Americans. Figures like Ida B. Wells and W.E.B. Du Bois challenged these racial dynamics through their writings and activism, raising awareness about the plight of those affected by sundown town policies. Their efforts laid the groundwork for future civil rights movements that sought to dismantle systemic racism across the nation.

The impact of sundown towns extends beyond their historical context into the modern racial dynamics of America. Many towns that were once sundown enclaves have retained their predominantly white demographics, leading to ongoing issues of racial inequality and segregation. The lingering effects of these discriminatory practices are evident in contemporary social relations, housing patterns, and access to resources. Understanding these historical events helps to illuminate the roots of racial tensions that continue to affect communities today.

Recognizing the legacy of sundown towns involves not only examining historical events and figures but also documenting personal narratives from descendants of both Black individuals who were expelled and white residents who lived in these towns. Their stories provide a more nuanced understanding of the social fabric that these towns created and the long-term consequences of their exclusionary practices. Educational programs aimed at addressing the legacy of sundown towns can foster dialogue and promote healing, encouraging communities to confront their past and work toward a more inclusive future.

The Decline of Sundown Towns

The decline of sundown towns in America marks a significant shift in the social and racial dynamics of many communities. Historically, these towns enforced a strict racial segregation policy, often through intimidation, violence, and discriminatory laws that required Black individuals to leave before sunset. As the civil rights movement gained momentum in the mid-20th century, the social fabric of these towns began to unravel. Activism, legal challenges, and changing public sentiments about race and equality contributed to the erosion of sundown town policies, leading to a gradual but unmistakable decline in their prevalence.

Legal changes played a pivotal role in dismantling the structures that upheld sundown towns. The Civil Rights Act of 1964 and subsequent legislation prohibited discrimination based on race, effectively nullifying the legal justifications for sundown town policies. Federal enforcement of these laws, along with the efforts of civil rights organizations, pressured local governments to abandon their exclusionary practices. Over time, many towns that once proudly displayed signs warning Black individuals to stay away began to confront their histories and reconsider their identities in a more inclusive manner.

Sociological impacts of this decline have been profound. As sundown towns opened their doors to people of color, they experienced demographic shifts that altered their cultural dynamics. Many communities began to embrace diversity, recognizing the economic and social benefits that come from a more inclusive population. However, this transition was not without resistance. In some areas, longstanding residents struggled to accept the changes, leading to tensions that reflected broader national conversations about race and identity. The legacy of sundown towns continues to influence community development, shaping how residents perceive their town's history and their role in fostering an inclusive environment.

In recent years, there has been a growing movement to document and preserve the histories of sundown towns. Local historians, activists, and educators have worked to unearth the narratives of those who lived in these communities, particularly the experiences of descendants of those who faced discrimination. Educational programs are being developed to address the legacy of sundown towns, fostering discussions about race, justice, and reconciliation. These initiatives aim to ensure that the lessons learned from the past are not forgotten and that future generations understand the importance of inclusivity and acceptance.

The decline of sundown towns reflects broader changes in American society regarding race and equality. While many towns have taken significant steps toward reconciliation and inclusivity, the remnants of their past still linger. Understanding this history is crucial in addressing contemporary racial dynamics and fostering a more equitable future. The journey from exclusion to inclusion is ongoing, and as communities confront their past, they have the opportunity to redefine their identities in ways that honor diversity and promote unity.

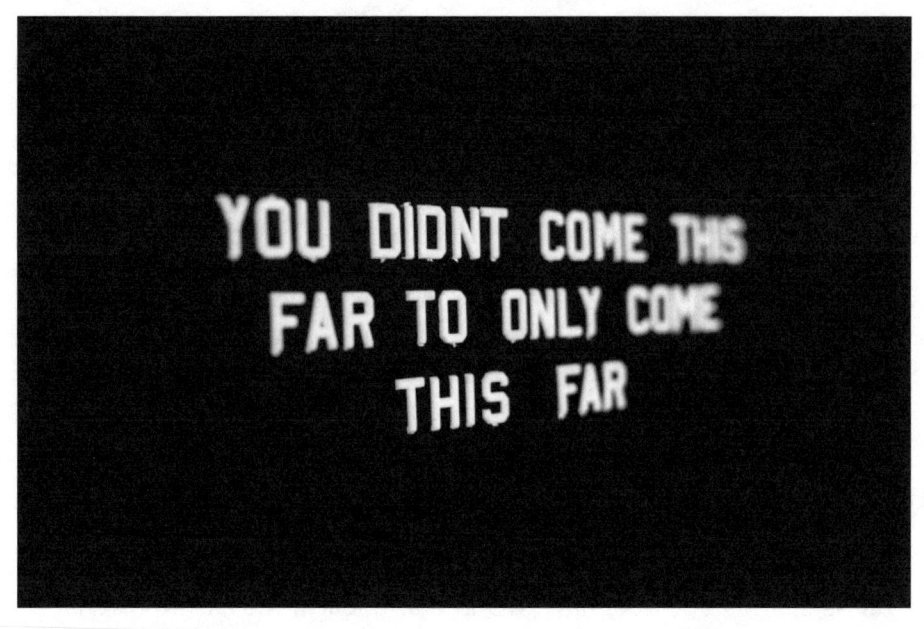

Chapter 3: Impact of Sundown Towns on Modern Racial Dynamics

Racial Segregation Today

Racial segregation continues to manifest in various forms across America today, showcasing a legacy that traces back to the era of sundown towns. These communities, which systematically excluded Black residents through a combination of legal restrictions and social intimidation, have left an indelible mark on the racial fabric of the nation. While many sundown towns have either transformed or faded from memory, the principles of exclusion and segregation remain alive in subtle yet impactful ways. The remnants of these policies can be observed in modern residential patterns, educational inequalities, and the persistent divide in law enforcement practices.

One of the most evident legacies of sundown towns is the ongoing residential segregation that characterizes many American cities. Areas that were once sundown towns often retain a demographic homogeneity that reflects their historical exclusionary practices. White flight and gentrification have further entrenched these divides, creating neighborhoods where the racial composition is starkly uneven.

This segregation is not merely a matter of preference but is frequently reinforced through real estate practices, zoning laws, and access to financial resources, thereby perpetuating a cycle of inequality that echoes the past.

Educational disparities are another critical aspect of modern racial segregation linked to the history of sundown towns. Schools in predominantly white neighborhoods often receive more funding and resources, resulting in better educational outcomes compared to schools in areas with higher populations of students of color. This inequity is compounded by the legacy of sundown towns, where historical exclusion has led to a concentration of poverty and a lack of investment in minority communities. Consequently, the educational system reflects broader societal inequalities, limiting opportunities for marginalized groups and perpetuating a cycle of disadvantage.

The influence of sundown towns is also evident in the practices of law enforcement. Communities that were once bastions of racial exclusion often exhibit patterns of policing that disproportionately target people of color. Racial profiling and excessive use of force have roots in the historical context of sundown towns, where the enforcement of segregation relied on intimidation and violence. This legacy continues to shape interactions between law enforcement and minority communities, fostering distrust and fear that hinder the quest for equitable justice.

As America moves towards 2025 and beyond, it is vital to recognize and confront the enduring impacts of sundown towns on racial dynamics today. Acknowledging this history encourages a more profound understanding of the contemporary issues of segregation and inequality. Educational initiatives aimed at highlighting the legacy of sundown towns can foster community dialogue and healing, ultimately paving the way for policies that promote inclusivity and equity. Only by confronting the shadows of the past can society hope to build a future that embraces diversity and dismantles the remnants of systemic segregation.

Economic Disparities and Opportunities

Economic disparities rooted in the legacy of sundown towns manifest in contemporary America through a complex interplay of historical injustices and modern opportunities. Sundown towns, which maintained racial homogeneity through discriminatory practices, have left lasting scars on their communities. These practices not only expelled Black residents but also stunted economic growth by limiting the diversity of the workforce and consumer base. As a result, many of these towns experience economic stagnation, characterized by lower property values and limited business opportunities, which stand in stark contrast to more diverse communities that benefit from a wider range of perspectives and innovations.

The lack of integration in sundown towns has created significant barriers to economic advancement for marginalized groups. In areas where Black individuals have historically been excluded, there are fewer opportunities for entrepreneurial ventures or access to quality education and employment. This systematic exclusion has repercussions that extend beyond individual communities, creating broader economic disparities that affect regional growth and development. Consequently, the historical context of sundown towns continues to shape the economic landscape, often leading to a cycle of poverty and disenfranchisement for those targeted by past discriminatory policies.

Despite these challenges, there are emerging opportunities for economic revitalization in areas previously marked by sundown town legacies. Efforts to diversify local economies by attracting businesses that prioritize inclusivity can lead to sustainable growth. Initiatives that encourage minority entrepreneurship and support local businesses can help bridge the economic divide. Furthermore, community engagement projects that involve diverse voices in decision-making processes can foster an environment where all residents feel valued and empowered to contribute to their local economies.

Education plays a pivotal role in addressing economic disparities linked to sundown town histories. Programs that focus on increasing awareness of the impacts of systemic racism and promoting financial literacy among historically marginalized groups can equip individuals with the tools needed to navigate and succeed in the modern economy. Additionally, partnerships between local governments, educational institutions, and community organizations can create pathways for job training and skill development, ensuring that previously excluded populations have access to opportunities that were once denied to them.

Ultimately, the legacy of sundown towns presents both a challenge and an opportunity for economic equity in modern America. Recognizing and addressing the historical injustices that have shaped economic disparities is crucial for fostering a more inclusive society. By embracing diversity and promoting equitable practices, communities can work towards dismantling the barriers created by the past, paving the way for a more prosperous future for all residents. As we move forward, it is essential to prioritize policies and initiatives that not only acknowledge these legacies but actively seek to rectify them, creating a landscape where everyone has the opportunity to thrive.

Interactions Between Communities

Interactions among communities, particularly those shaped by the legacy of sundown towns, reveal a complex tapestry of historical tensions and contemporary relationships. While sundown towns were explicitly designed to exclude Black residents through laws and violence, the interactions that took place during the day, when Black individuals were allowed to work and shop, established a unique dynamic. These encounters often reflected a facade of coexistence, where economic necessity temporarily masked underlying racial animosities. In many cases, Black individuals were seen as essential to the local economy during daylight hours, yet their presence was largely tolerated rather than welcomed, laying the groundwork for ongoing racial disparities.

The legacy of these communities continues to influence interactions today. As towns grapple with their histories, many face the challenge of reconciling past injustices with the desire for a more inclusive future. In some instances, descendants of sundown towns have initiated dialogues with neighboring communities and organizations to confront this history. These conversations often center around acknowledgment of past wrongs, fostering an environment of healing and understanding. However, the effectiveness of these interactions can be hampered by long-standing prejudices and the reluctance of some residents to engage with uncomfortable truths about their community's past.

Moreover, the interactions between historically white communities and those still predominantly Black or diverse today often reveal the lingering effects of sundown town legacies. The economic relationships established in the past do not always translate into equitable social interactions in the present. For example, while Black residents may participate in local economies, systemic barriers often limit their full integration into community life. This can manifest in social networks that are still racially segmented, where trust and mutual support may be lacking due to historical grievances. Such divisions complicate community cohesion and hinder collective progress toward equity and inclusion.

Law enforcement has historically played a significant role in the interactions within sundown towns, further entrenching racial divides. The presence of police in these communities often served to reinforce the boundaries initially established by sundown laws. To this day, the relationship between law enforcement and marginalized communities remains fraught, as incidents of racial profiling and discrimination continue to evoke fears reminiscent of past injustices. Efforts to reform policing practices are essential to fostering healthier interactions among all community members and addressing the legacy of mistrust that persists in the wake of sundown town histories.

Ultimately, addressing the interactions between communities shaped by a sundown town legacy requires a multifaceted approach. Educational programs aimed at increasing awareness about the historical context of these towns can play a crucial role in reshaping perceptions. By highlighting personal narratives from descendants of both Black individuals who were excluded and white residents who lived in these towns, communities can foster empathy and understanding. Through open dialogues, informed by a commitment to acknowledging the past, communities can work toward building bridges, promoting inclusivity, and creating a shared future that honors the diverse legacies of all residents.

Chapter 4: Case Studies of Sundown Towns: Past and Present

Notable Sundown Towns: A Historical Overview

Notable sundown towns across the United States serve as stark reminders of a darker chapter in American history, where racial segregation was enforced through both legal means and social intimidation. One of the most infamous examples is Martinsville, Indiana, where a sign at the town's entrance declared that Black individuals had to leave by sundown. This town epitomized the violent enforcement of racial boundaries, with reports of lynchings and other acts of terror directed at those who dared to defy the unwritten rules. The legacy of Martinsville is not merely a relic; it continues to shape the community's demographics and racial dynamics to this day.

Another significant example is the town of Anna, Illinois, which was marked by its aggressive policies against Black residents. The enforcement of sundown laws in Anna was not just limited to signs; it involved organized groups that would patrol the streets to ensure compliance. This not only created an atmosphere of fear for Black individuals but also led to a long-standing stigma that has affected the town's reputation. Even decades after such practices ceased, the remnants of this history influence perceptions and interactions among residents, demonstrating how deeply ingrained these prejudices can become.

In the West, cities like Oroville, California, present a different yet equally troubling narrative. Although the methods of enforcement may have differed, the underlying principles of exclusion remained consistent. Oroville's history reflects the broader trends of racial segregation that were often justified under the guise of community safety and moral standards. This town, like many others, has faced challenges in reconciling its past with its present, often grappling with the legacies of racism that linger in public consciousness and community identity.

The impact of these sundown towns extends beyond historical significance; they have left indelible marks on modern racial dynamics. In many instances, the demographic shifts that occurred as a result of these exclusionary practices have led to lasting socioeconomic disparities. Communities that once enforced sundown policies often struggle with issues of economic development and social cohesion, as the scars of their past inhibit progress toward inclusivity. This ongoing struggle underscores the importance of understanding the historical context in which these towns operated.

Efforts to document and preserve the histories of notable sundown towns are crucial for fostering awareness and education about their legacies. Initiatives aimed at addressing these histories through local museums, educational programs, and community discussions are essential in promoting healing and reconciliation. By exploring the complexities of these towns, both past and present, society can better understand the pervasive nature of racism and work towards dismantling the barriers it has created, ultimately paving the way for a more equitable future.

Contemporary Sundown Towns

Contemporary sundown towns represent a complex and often troubling legacy in modern America, where the remnants of discriminatory practices still echo in community dynamics and racial relations. While the overt legal restrictions that defined these towns have largely been dismantled, the social and psychological impact of their history lingers. Many communities that once enforced sundown policies may not openly acknowledge their past, yet the effects of systemic racism continue to shape interactions among residents and influence the demographics of these areas.

In examining the characteristics of contemporary sundown towns, it is evident that the historical framework of exclusion persists in various forms. Although the explicit expulsion of Black individuals is no longer legally sanctioned, subtle mechanisms such as discriminatory housing practices, economic disparities, and social ostracism can create environments that feel unwelcoming to people of color. These subtleties often manifest in the form of informal agreements among residents, unspoken rules governing community behavior, and a reluctance to engage with diversity, effectively maintaining a racially homogeneous atmosphere.

The impact of sundown towns on modern racial dynamics can be observed in the ongoing challenges faced by communities striving for inclusivity. Many towns that historically excluded Black residents still struggle with the legacy of mistrust and fear. For instance, Black individuals and families seeking to move into these areas often encounter significant barriers, including racial profiling, higher scrutiny in housing applications, and a lack of support from local institutions. This creates a cycle where the absence of diverse perspectives further entrenches the existing social fabric, leading to a stagnation of cultural growth and understanding.

Case studies of specific towns illustrate how the past continues to shape the present. Some communities have attempted to confront their histories by engaging in dialogues about racial equity and justice, while others remain in denial, clinging to the status quo. These case studies reveal a spectrum of responses, from towns that have embraced diversity and actively worked to dismantle their sundown town legacies to those that resist change and perpetuate a culture of exclusion. The outcomes of these efforts highlight the importance of community engagement and the willingness to confront uncomfortable truths.

Educational programs addressing the legacy of sundown towns play a critical role in shaping future generations' understanding of race and community. By providing resources and training for both educators and students, these programs aim to foster awareness of the historical context and its implications for modern society. The promotion of inclusive narratives can help dismantle the historical amnesia that often surrounds sundown towns, encouraging dialogue and understanding among residents. As communities navigate their complex histories, the commitment to education and reconciliation becomes essential in moving toward a more equitable future.

Lessons Learned from Case Studies

The examination of sundown towns through case studies offers critical insights into the persistence of racial dynamics in contemporary America. Each case serves as a microcosm of broader societal issues, illustrating how historical practices of exclusion have lasting impacts on community development, race relations, and legal frameworks. By analyzing specific examples, such as the experiences in places like Anna, Illinois, and other sundown towns, we can better understand the mechanisms that sustained these communities and the ways they continue to shape modern society.

One significant lesson learned from these case studies is the importance of public memory and historical acknowledgment. Many towns have begun to confront their pasts, recognizing the harm caused by discriminatory practices. This reckoning often involves efforts to document histories, preserve narratives, and educate current residents about the legacies of exclusion. By fostering an environment of remembrance, communities can begin to heal and work toward reconciliation, acknowledging the pain inflicted on marginalized groups while also promoting a more inclusive identity.

Another prominent theme that emerges is the role of local governance in perpetuating or dismantling these legacies. Case studies illustrate how municipal policies and law enforcement practices were historically aligned with maintaining racial homogeneity. This has implications for understanding current governance structures and the need for reform. By examining how local laws were enforced, particularly regarding policing and community standards, we can identify patterns that persist today, allowing for more informed discussions about equitable policy-making.

The impact of sundown towns on modern racial dynamics cannot be overstated.
These case studies reveal a pattern of segregation that extends beyond the boundaries of the towns themselves. The lasting effects of exclusionary practices contribute to residential segregation, economic disparities, and social stratification in nearby urban areas. Understanding these connections is essential for addressing contemporary issues of inequality and fostering a more equitable society, as the legacy of sundown towns continues to influence the lived experiences of racial minorities.

Lastly, personal narratives from descendants of residents in sundown towns provide powerful testimony to the enduring effects of these historical injustices. These stories highlight the emotional and psychological toll on individuals and families, illustrating how the legacy of exclusion can shape identity and community ties. Engaging with these narratives is vital for fostering empathy and understanding, encouraging all members of society to confront uncomfortable truths about the past while working together toward a more inclusive future.

22

Chapter 5: Legal Frameworks Surrounding Sundown Towns

Historical Legislation and Sundown Towns

Historical legislation played a crucial role in the establishment and perpetuation of sundown towns across the United States. These communities enforced racial homogeneity through a combination of local ordinances, state laws, and social customs, which collectively aimed to exclude Black individuals and other minorities from residing within their borders. In the late 19th and early 20th centuries, as white populations sought to maintain control over local demographics, various laws were enacted that effectively barred Black residents from settling in, or even visiting, these towns after dark. These legislative measures were often couched in the language of public safety, property values, and community integrity, masking the underlying intent of racial exclusion.

The enforcement of sundown town policies was not solely a matter of written law. In many cases, local law enforcement and vigilante groups actively participated in the intimidation and expulsion of Black individuals. This extrajudicial enforcement was often brutal, with reports of violence and threats aimed at those who dared to remain in or return to these towns after sunset. The culture of fear and hostility created an environment where Black individuals understood that their presence would not be tolerated, thus reinforcing the unwritten rules of these communities. As a result, the legacy of these practices left deep scars on both the towns that embraced such policies and the communities that were systematically excluded.

Legislation designed to protect civil rights, such as the Civil Rights Act of 1964, sought to dismantle the structures that allowed sundown towns to thrive. However, the enforcement of these laws was often weak, and many sundown towns continued to operate in a manner that excluded Black residents. Moreover, the legacy of sundown towns persisted long after the laws changed. The social and economic impacts of these towns created lasting divisions, influencing educational opportunities, housing availability, and community resources for generations. As such, the historical legislation that allowed sundown towns to flourish did not simply disappear; it evolved and transformed, leaving a complex legacy that still influences racial dynamics today.

Modern examinations of sundown towns reveal the lingering effects of historical legislation on community development and racial relations. Case studies of towns that were once sundown communities show that, despite legal changes, the social fabric of these areas often retains echoes of their exclusionary past. Many towns still grapple with issues of racial segregation, limited diversity, and unequal access to resources. These dynamics contribute to a broader understanding of how historical policies

24

shape contemporary realities, as well as the ongoing struggle for racial equality in areas once defined by exclusion.

As the conversation about sundown towns continues, it is essential to recognize the importance of documenting and preserving the histories of these communities. Educational programs addressing the legacy of sundown towns can play a vital role in fostering awareness and promoting dialogue about race and inclusion. By exploring the historical legislation that enabled these towns and understanding their enduring impact, communities can begin to confront the shadows of their past and work toward a more equitable future. This journey requires a collective effort to acknowledge the injustices of history while striving to build inclusive spaces for all individuals, regardless of their racial or ethnic backgrounds.

Modern Legal Challenges

Modern legal challenges arising from the legacy of sundown towns are complex and multifaceted. As communities grapple with the historical implications of these racially exclusive practices, the legal systems in place must contend with the remnants of discriminatory laws and policies that have perpetuated systemic racism. One of the most pressing issues is the enforcement of civil rights laws that aim to dismantle the lingering impacts of sundown town policies. While significant legislative advancements have been made, such as the Fair Housing Act and the Civil Rights Act, the real-world application of these laws often falls short, particularly in towns with entrenched racial biases.

Another significant challenge lies in the documentation and recognition of sundown towns within legal frameworks. Many communities have yet to acknowledge their histories as sundown towns, leading to a lack of comprehensive legal accountability for past actions. This denial not only affects the ability of descendants to seek reparations or justice but also complicates efforts to ensure that such discriminatory practices are not repeated. Advocates argue that a formal acknowledgment of these histories is crucial for advancing legal reforms that can address current inequities rooted in this legacy.

Litigation has emerged as a tool for addressing these historical grievances, yet it often faces obstacles in proving the connection between past discriminatory practices and contemporary racial disparities. Courts may struggle to recognize the long-term impacts of sundown town policies on current populations, particularly in cases involving housing discrimination, economic disparity, and social exclusion. As a result, legal challenges in this arena frequently require innovative approaches to bridge historical injustices with modern legal standards.

The role of local governments and law enforcement agencies also presents a significant challenge. In many cases, these institutions were complicit in the enforcement of sundown town policies, creating an atmosphere of mistrust among marginalized communities. Efforts to reform law enforcement practices and increase accountability are essential, yet they often meet resistance from those who may not fully understand or acknowledge the historical context of these issues. Building trust and fostering constructive dialogue between law enforcement and communities impacted by the legacy of sundown towns is vital for effective legal and social reform.

Finally, educational initiatives play a crucial role in addressing modern legal challenges associated with sundown towns. By raising awareness about the historical and ongoing impacts of these communities, educational programs can empower individuals to advocate for change and hold local governments accountable. As more people become informed about the legacy of sundown towns, there is potential for a collective movement toward justice and equity. However, without sustained effort and legal commitment, the shadows of the past may continue to haunt modern America, perpetuating cycles of inequality and discrimination.

The Role of Civil Rights Laws

The role of civil rights laws in addressing the legacy of sundown towns is a critical aspect of understanding the ongoing racial dynamics in America. Civil rights legislation emerged as a response to the systemic discrimination faced by African Americans, particularly in communities that were historically characterized by exclusionary practices. Laws such as the Civil Rights Act of 1964 and the Fair Housing Act of 1968 aimed to dismantle the legal frameworks that allowed sundown towns to thrive. These laws sought to ensure that all individuals, regardless of race, would have equal access to public spaces, housing, and employment opportunities, thereby challenging the very foundations upon which sundown towns were built.

The enforcement of civil rights laws has had a significant impact on the visibility and operation of sundown towns. While many sundown towns have not officially existed in legal terms since the mid-20th century, the remnants of their policies continue to influence community dynamics. The introduction of legal repercussions for discriminatory practices forced many communities to confront their past. However, the effectiveness of these laws often depended on local enforcement and community willingness to change, resulting in a patchwork of progress across the country. In some areas, the legacy of exclusion still lingers, as old habits die hard and the societal norms established by sundown towns continue to inform interactions among residents.

The passage of civil rights laws also opened avenues for litigation against the overt and covert practices that perpetuated racial segregation. Legal cases brought forth by civil rights organizations have highlighted the ongoing discrimination faced by individuals in areas formerly designated as sundown towns. These cases not only serve to hold communities accountable but also to educate the public about the historical context of these towns and their lasting impact. The process of legal redress has reinforced the idea that communities must reckon with their past to create a more equitable future.

Furthermore, civil rights laws have paved the way for educational initiatives that address the legacy of sundown towns. Schools and community organizations are increasingly incorporating historical analyses of racial segregation into their curricula, fostering a deeper understanding of the implications that sundown towns have had on modern society. This educational emphasis aims to cultivate a generation that is aware of the historical injustices and motivated to advocate for inclusive policies. By acknowledging the past, communities can better navigate the complexities of their current racial dynamics and work towards healing and reconciliation.

Ultimately, the role of civil rights laws in the context of sundown towns is emblematic of the broader struggle for racial equality in America. While these laws have provided essential tools for challenging discrimination, the enduring effects of sundown towns highlight the need for ongoing vigilance and advocacy. As society moves forward, it is crucial to remain aware of the historical constructs that continue to shape contemporary communities, ensuring that the lessons learned from the era of sundown towns inform efforts to build a more just and inclusive society for all.

Chapter 6: Personal Narratives from Descendants of Sundown Town Residents

Stories of Displacement and Resilience

The history of sundown towns is marked by stories of displacement and resilience that reveal the complex interplay of racial dynamics in America. These towns, often characterized by their exclusionary practices, forced African Americans to navigate a landscape fraught with danger and hostility. The expulsion of Black residents was not merely a historical footnote; it was a systematic effort to maintain white supremacy through intimidation and violence. Individuals who dared to challenge these boundaries often faced severe repercussions, reinforcing the notion that safety and belonging were privileges reserved for white citizens.

Despite the oppressive environment, many African Americans displayed remarkable resilience in the face of adversity. They created networks of support and solidarity, often relying on family ties and communal bonds to endure the psychological and physical toll of living in or near sundown towns. These informal networks played a critical role in providing resources, information, and safe passage during the daylight hours, allowing individuals to access jobs and services while avoiding the dangers that lurked after dusk. The courage and ingenuity displayed by these communities highlight a spirit that resisted the narrative of defeat often associated with displacement.

The legacies of these experiences continue to impact modern racial dynamics, as descendants of those who lived through these oppressive periods grapple with the historical weight of their family histories. Personal narratives from those whose ancestors were directly affected by sundown town policies reveal a complex tapestry of trauma and triumph. Many descendants carry forward the stories of resilience, using their platforms to educate others about the historical injustices that have shaped their communities. This act of remembrance not only honors the struggles of the past but also serves as a catalyst for change in the present.

The sociological impacts of sundown towns extend beyond individual stories; they have shaped community development and social structures in profound ways. The division created by these discriminatory practices has fostered a legacy of mistrust and segregation that persists in various forms today. Understanding these dynamics is crucial for addressing ongoing racial disparities and fostering more inclusive communities. By examining the historical context of these towns, we can begin to unravel the complex layers of systemic racism that continue to influence societal interactions.

Educational programs that address the legacy of sundown towns play a vital role in fostering awareness and dialogue around these issues. By integrating stories of displacement and resilience into curricula, educators can challenge students to confront uncomfortable truths about race and community in America. These programs not only aim to preserve the histories of those affected but also encourage critical thinking about the ongoing implications of these legacies in contemporary society. Through education, we can cultivate a deeper understanding of our past, ultimately paving the way for a more equitable future.

The Impact of Legacy on Current Generations

The legacy of sundown towns continues to cast a long shadow over modern American society, influencing the dynamics of race relations and community identity. As the descendants of those who lived in these towns grapple with the past, the remnants of exclusionary practices can still be felt today. This legacy manifests not only in the memories and narratives passed down through generations but also in the socio-economic structures that have been shaped by historical injustices. Understanding how these past injustices affect current generations is crucial for addressing the systemic inequalities that persist in many communities.

In many cases, the impact of sundown towns is evident in the demographics of contemporary neighborhoods. The racial homogeneity that was once enforced through intimidation and violence has lasting effects on community interactions and the socio-economic opportunities available to minority groups. Areas that were once sundown towns often retain a white majority, contributing to an environment where cultural diversity is limited, and racial biases may be perpetuated. This lack of diversity can hinder empathy and understanding between different racial groups, making it difficult to address issues of inequality and discrimination effectively.

The psychological effects of living in a sundown town have also influenced modern communities. Descendants of residents who upheld these exclusionary practices may internalize prejudices or face guilt and shame regarding their family's legacy. Conversely, those from marginalized backgrounds may carry the burden of historical trauma, impacting their sense of belonging and agency within these towns. The narratives surrounding sundown towns serve as a reminder of the need for reconciliation and healing, emphasizing the importance of acknowledging history as a means of fostering understanding and inclusivity among different generations.

Moreover, the legal frameworks surrounding sundown towns have evolved, yet many remnants of discriminatory policies persist in subtle forms, such as zoning laws and housing regulations. These systems can perpetuate inequalities and reinforce the socio-economic divides that began with the sundown town phenomenon. Recognizing the historical context of these laws is essential for contemporary policy-making, as it allows for a more nuanced approach to addressing racial disparities and fostering equitable communities. Efforts to dismantle systemic racism must be informed by an understanding of how past injustices continue to shape the present.

Finally, educational programs aimed at addressing the legacy of sundown towns play a vital role in shaping the understanding of current generations. By incorporating the history of these towns into school curricula and community discussions, we can foster awareness and dialogue about racial issues. Such initiatives encourage reflection on the past and promote a collective commitment to creating more inclusive communities. It is through education and open conversations about legacy that present and future generations can begin to dismantle the barriers created by a history of exclusion and embrace a more equitable society.

Voices from the Community

In examining the legacy of sundown towns, it is crucial to amplify the voices of community members who have experienced the lingering effects of these racially exclusive practices. Their stories offer profound insights into the ongoing impact of historical injustices. Many residents recall tales passed down through generations, recounting the fear and intimidation that shaped their neighborhoods. These narratives illuminate how the echoes of past discrimination continue to influence modern social dynamics and community interactions.

Community members often reflect on the contradictions inherent in sundown towns. While some residents express pride in their town's history and development, others acknowledge the discomfort that arises from recognizing the exclusionary practices that once defined their community. This duality contributes to a complex identity, where individuals grapple with the shame of the past while striving to foster inclusivity in the present. Such discussions are vital for understanding how historical legacies shape contemporary values and attitudes toward race.

The personal narratives of descendants of sundown town residents reveal the emotional burden carried by those who inherit a history of exclusion. For many, the legacy of their ancestors' actions creates a sense of responsibility to confront and address these issues. Interviews with these individuals often highlight their commitment to advocacy and education, aiming to dismantle the barriers that sundown town legacies have erected. This intergenerational dialogue fosters a deeper understanding of the past, empowering newer generations to promote change and healing.

In addition, community forums and local initiatives have emerged to confront the realities of sundown town histories. Residents are increasingly engaging in discussions about the implications of their town's past, creating spaces for reconciliation and awareness. These efforts often include collaborative projects focused on preserving the histories of marginalized groups and ensuring that the stories of those affected by sundown town policies are not forgotten. By acknowledging these voices, communities can work toward developing a more inclusive narrative that honors all residents.

Ultimately, the voices from the community serve as a powerful reminder of the importance of collective memory in shaping

a more equitable future. By listening to the experiences of those impacted by the legacy of sundown towns, society can better understand the complexities of racial dynamics and work towards healing and unity. These stories not only reflect the painful past but also inspire action and commitment to creating inclusive environments where all individuals can thrive, free from the shadows of discrimination.

Chapter 7: Sociological Impacts of Sundown Towns

on Community Development

Community Identity and Cohesion

Community identity in sundown towns has evolved significantly over the years, shaped by the historical context of racial segregation and exclusion. These towns were often marked by a collective memory that valorized a homogeneous community, fostering a sense of pride among residents who identified strongly with their shared racial background. This identity was reinforced through social institutions and local traditions, creating a narrative that positioned the community as a bastion of safety and purity against perceived threats from outside groups. The exclusionary practices that defined these towns, while rooted in racism, also contributed to a tightly-knit community where conformity was valued, and dissent was often silenced.

Cohesion within sundown towns was frequently bolstered by a shared understanding of the community's racial policies and norms. Residents collaborated to maintain the status quo, which included informal agreements on who could live, work, and socialize within the town's borders. This cohesion often manifested in social gatherings, local governance, and even economic practices that favored white residents. The exclusion of Black individuals was not merely a matter of personal prejudice but a collective endeavor that created a sense of belonging among those who adhered to the unwritten rules of the town.

The legacy of sundown towns continues to impact community cohesion today. Modern residents, whether aware or unaware of their town's history, may find themselves influenced by the long-standing racial dynamics that have shaped their community's identity. In some cases, this has led to a reluctance to embrace diversity, as the historical narrative remains embedded in the social fabric. As a result, communities that once prided themselves on their racial homogeneity may struggle with the challenges posed by demographic changes, often leading to tension between long-standing residents and newcomers.

However, the path toward healing and rebuilding community identity is not without hope. Many towns are beginning to confront their past, engaging in difficult conversations about race and inclusion. Initiatives aimed at documenting and preserving the histories of these towns have emerged, allowing for a fuller understanding of both the harm caused by exclusionary practices and the resilience of those who suffered under them. Educational programs focused on the legacy of sundown towns are fostering awareness and encouraging community members to embrace a more inclusive identity that acknowledges the past while looking toward a more equitable future.

Ultimately, the journey toward redefining community identity and cohesion in the wake of sundown town legacies requires a commitment to understanding and addressing historical injustices. It calls for fostering dialogue, promoting inclusivity, and cultivating a sense of belonging for all residents, regardless of their racial or ethnic backgrounds. By recognizing the impact of their history, communities can begin to dismantle the barriers that have long divided them and work towards a collective identity that celebrates diversity and shared humanity.

Social Stratification and Inequality

Social stratification and inequality are deeply rooted in the historical context of sundown towns, which were established as safe havens for white populations at the expense of Black communities. These towns utilized a combination of legal restrictions, social norms, and outright violence to maintain their all-white status. This deliberate exclusion created a hierarchical structure within society, where access to resources, opportunities, and even basic rights was determined by race. The legacy of these practices continues to shape modern American society, perpetuating economic disparities and social divisions.

The enforcement mechanisms of sundown towns were particularly insidious. While Black individuals could work and shop during daylight hours, they faced the constant threat of violence if they remained after dark. This enforced curfew not only served as a tool of racial control but also instilled a pervasive culture of fear. The psychological impact of such intimidation has reverberated through generations, contributing to ongoing social isolation and economic challenges for affected communities. In essence, sundown towns created an environment where racial hierarchies were normalized and codified, laying the groundwork for systemic inequality.

The historical analysis of sundown towns reveals the ways in which law enforcement played a significant role in maintaining these discriminatory practices. Police often acted as enforcers of racial segregation, either turning a blind eye to violence against Black individuals or actively participating in their expulsion. This complicity reinforced the idea that certain communities were inherently superior to others, further entrenching social stratification. The legacy of these actions is still felt today, as many communities grapple with distrust towards law enforcement and the implications of a racially biased justice system.

Modern racial dynamics are also influenced by the historical existence of sundown towns. The physical and psychological barriers established in these communities have created lasting effects on the social fabric of America. Areas that were once sundown towns often continue to experience economic decline, limited access to education, and marginalized populations. The disparities in wealth and opportunity reflect a broader pattern of inequality that stems from these historical injustices, perpetuating cycles of disadvantage for marginalized groups.

Addressing the legacy of sundown towns requires a multifaceted approach that acknowledges the role of social stratification and inequality in shaping contemporary society. Educational programs that focus on the history and impact of these towns can foster a better understanding of racial dynamics and encourage dialogue among diverse community members. By recognizing the historical context of racial exclusion, communities can begin to dismantle the structures of inequality and work towards a more equitable future, ensuring that the shadows of the past do not continue to dictate the paths of the present and future.

The Role of Education in Social Development

Education plays a pivotal role in social development, particularly in the context of communities previously characterized as sundown towns. The legacy of these towns, where discriminatory practices were normalized, continues to affect social dynamics today. Education serves as a crucial tool for awareness and understanding, facilitating the dismantling of the prejudices that once defined these communities. By integrating comprehensive histories of sundown towns into educational curricula, students can cultivate a greater understanding of the past and its implications for present and future societal interactions.

The inclusion of sundown town histories in education can foster critical discussions about race, privilege, and community responsibility. As students learn about the historical context of these towns, they can begin to recognize the systems of oppression that allowed such segregation to flourish. This awareness can empower individuals to challenge discriminatory practices and promote inclusivity in their own communities. Educational institutions have the unique opportunity to serve as platforms for dialogue, encouraging students to confront uncomfortable truths about their local histories and the ongoing impact of these legacies.

Furthermore, education can facilitate the development of empathy and understanding among diverse populations. Programs that engage students in discussions about the personal narratives of individuals affected by sundown town policies can humanize the historical context. When students hear the stories of those who experienced exclusion and violence, it fosters a sense of connection and responsibility to advocate for social justice. Empathetic understanding is essential for building bridges across racial and cultural divides, ultimately contributing to a more cohesive society.

In addition to historical awareness, education can also promote community engagement and activism. Schools and educational programs can encourage students to participate in initiatives that address the lingering effects of sundown town histories. By involving youth in community service projects, workshops, and discussions on equity, educators can inspire the next generation of leaders to actively work towards dismantling systemic racism. This proactive approach enables students to apply their learning in meaningful ways, cultivating a sense of agency in shaping their communities.

Lastly, the evolution of educational frameworks must prioritize inclusivity and representation. As we move towards 2025 and beyond, it is crucial for educational institutions to reflect on their curricula and ensure that they adequately represent the histories and contributions of marginalized communities. By valuing diverse perspectives and experiences, education can play a transformative role in social development, fostering environments that reject the legacies of sundown towns and embrace a future grounded in equity and respect for all.

Chapter 8: The Role of Law Enforcement in Sundown Towns

Historical Functions of Law Enforcement

The historical functions of law enforcement in sundown towns reveal a complex interplay between societal norms and systemic racism. Law enforcement agencies were often complicit in maintaining the status quo of racial segregation and discrimination. In many cases, officers were not just enforcers of the law but also active participants in upholding the community's racial boundaries. Their presence served to intimidate Black individuals who dared to remain in the town after dark, reinforcing the notion that these spaces were exclusively for white residents. This dynamic was not merely a local phenomenon; it reflected broader national policies and attitudes towards race and law enforcement.

In sundown towns, law enforcement's primary function extended beyond traditional crime prevention. Officers often acted as gatekeepers to maintain the racial purity of the community. They would patrol neighborhoods, ensuring that Black individuals were removed before sunset. This policing strategy involved direct confrontations, where officers could use threats or violence to expel Black residents or visitors. This function was legitimized by a legal framework that tolerated or even encouraged such discriminatory practices, effectively criminalizing the mere presence of Black individuals in these areas.

The enforcement of sundown policies by law enforcement had far-reaching implications for community dynamics. The fear instilled by police presence created an environment where Black individuals were discouraged from seeking refuge or employment. This not only perpetuated economic disparities but also fostered an atmosphere of mistrust between communities and law enforcement. In towns where law enforcement was seen as a protector of white interests, the policing practices served to alienate Black communities further and reinforce racial divisions that continue to affect societal interactions today.

Moreover, the historical functions of law enforcement in sundown towns also illustrate the challenges of accountability and justice in racially charged environments. Officers who engaged in discriminatory practices often faced little to no repercussions, as their actions aligned with the prevailing social order. Consequently, the lack of oversight allowed for a culture of impunity, where racial violence could flourish under the guise of law enforcement. This legacy persists in contemporary discussions about police practices, as communities grapple with the ongoing impact of these historical injustices.

Understanding the historical functions of law enforcement in sundown towns is crucial for recognizing the roots of modern racial dynamics. As we analyze the past, it becomes clear that the actions of law enforcement in these communities were not isolated incidents but part of a larger system of oppression. Acknowledging this history is essential for fostering dialogue about racial equity and justice today. By examining how law enforcement has been wielded as a tool for maintaining racial segregation, we can better understand the complexities of current law enforcement practices and their implications for marginalized communities.

Current Law Enforcement Practices

Current law enforcement practices in America continue to grapple with the legacy of sundown towns, where historical enforcement of racial exclusion has left deep scars on communities. In many regions, the remnants of these towns still affect interactions between law enforcement and marginalized groups. Police practices often reflect the historical prejudices that were once codified into law, leading to a complicated relationship between law enforcement agencies and the very communities they are tasked with protecting. This legacy manifests in various forms, from biased policing methods to the underreporting of crimes committed against people of color.

One prominent characteristic of contemporary law enforcement in areas formerly designated as sundown towns is the reliance on community policing strategies. While these strategies aim to foster better relationships between police and residents, they can inadvertently echo past practices. In some cases, law enforcement officers are seen as representatives of an authority that historically enforced racial segregation and violence. This perception can hinder trust-building efforts, as community members may remain wary of police involvement, fearing a resurgence of discriminatory practices that were prevalent in their towns' histories.

Moreover, the enforcement of laws against day-time presence of people of color in areas that were once sundown towns has evolved into modern forms of racial profiling and discrimination. Law enforcement agencies often face criticism for disproportionately targeting individuals based on race, a practice that raises questions about the motivations behind such actions. The legacy of sundown towns contributes to a climate where racial prejudice can influence decision-making, leading to misunderstandings and escalating tensions between law enforcement and communities of color.

As a response to these challenges, there is a growing emphasis on training programs that address implicit bias and historical context in law enforcement practices. Many departments are beginning to implement educational initiatives aimed at fostering a deeper understanding of the social and historical factors that shape contemporary racial dynamics. These programs are crucial in helping officers recognize the long-standing impacts of sundown town policies and in developing more equitable approaches to policing that prioritize community engagement and respect for all residents.

Ultimately, the evolution of law enforcement practices in areas with a history of sundown towns reflects a broader societal struggle to confront and rectify the injustices of the past. The ongoing dialogue about policing, race, and community relations reveals the complexities of addressing historical wrongs while striving for a more inclusive future. As communities work toward healing and reconciliation, the role of law enforcement will be pivotal in shaping new, constructive relationships that honor the legacy of those who suffered under discriminatory practices while fostering safety and justice for all.

The Relationship Between Law Enforcement and Communities

The relationship between law enforcement and communities, particularly in the context of sundown towns, reflects a complex interplay of power, fear, and historical legacy. In many sundown towns, law enforcement was not merely a protective presence but often a tool for enforcing racial segregation and intimidation. Officers would patrol neighborhoods with the explicit purpose of ensuring that Black individuals were not present after dark, often using aggressive tactics to expel those who defied these unwritten rules. This dynamic created an environment where the police were seen more as enforcers of racial boundaries than as protectors of all community members.

In contemporary discussions, the impact of this historical relationship continues to resonate. Communities that once systematically excluded Black individuals now grapple with the long-term effects of this exclusion on trust and cooperation with law enforcement. In many cases, descendants of those who lived in sundown towns express mistrust towards police due to the historical actions of their predecessors. This mistrust can hinder effective collaboration between law enforcement and communities, complicating efforts to address crime and ensure public safety. Understanding this history is crucial for both community members and law enforcement agencies aiming to rebuild relationships.

Moreover, the role of law enforcement in sundown towns often extended beyond the mere enforcement of curfews and racial boundaries. Many police departments were complicit in acts of violence and intimidation that were aimed at maintaining the status quo. This complicity fostered a culture of silence and fear, where victims of racial violence were often unwilling to seek help from those sworn to protect them. The lasting consequences of this complicity contribute to ongoing tensions in modern communities that must confront their histories while striving for a more equitable future.

The evolution of law enforcement's role in these communities over time illustrates shifts in societal attitudes and legal frameworks. As civil rights movements gained momentum, the expectation for police to serve all community members began to emerge. However, the transition has not been smooth, and many communities still bear the scars of their past. Law enforcement agencies today are challenged to reconcile their historical roles with current demands for accountability, transparency, and community engagement. This ongoing process is essential for healing and rebuilding trust between police and communities historically impacted by systemic racism.

Ultimately, the relationship between law enforcement and communities in sundown towns serves as a powerful reminder of the legacy of racial segregation in America. Addressing this legacy requires not only acknowledging the past but also actively working towards restorative practices that foster understanding and collaboration. Community-based initiatives, educational programs, and open dialogues about history and its impact on present-day interactions are critical steps in redefining this relationship. Only through such concerted efforts can communities hope to overcome the shadows of their past and move towards a more inclusive future.

Chapter 9: Documentation and Preservation of Sundown Town Histories

Archiving Historical Records

Archiving historical records related to sundown towns is essential for understanding the legacy of these communities and their lasting impact on American society. The preservation of documents, photographs, oral histories, and legal records is crucial for creating a comprehensive narrative of the policies and practices that maintained racial segregation and discrimination. Archives serve not only as repositories of information but also as tools for education, allowing future generations to learn about the injustices faced by marginalized communities. By documenting the experiences of those who lived in sundown towns, historians and researchers can provide insight into the mechanisms of exclusion and the societal structures that allowed such practices to flourish.

The process of archiving involves careful curation and organization of materials that reflect the realities of sundown towns. This includes collecting evidence of local laws that enforced segregation, personal accounts from residents, and reports of violence and intimidation faced by Black individuals. Digital archiving has become increasingly important, as it allows for broader access to these records by researchers, educators, and the general public. The digitization of documents not only preserves fragile materials but also enhances their visibility, ensuring that the stories of these towns are not lost to time. Online databases and virtual exhibits can provide a platform for sharing these histories with a wider audience, fostering a deeper understanding of the racial dynamics that persist today.

In addition to traditional archival methods, community engagement plays a vital role in the preservation of sundown town histories. Collaborations with local organizations and descendants of former residents can yield rich oral histories and personal narratives that are often absent from official records. These stories add depth and context to the historical data, highlighting the lived experiences of those affected by sundown town policies. Engaging communities in the archiving process not only empowers individuals to reclaim their narratives but also fosters a sense of responsibility to remember and educate others about the past. Workshops, local history projects, and collaborative research initiatives can facilitate these connections and encourage active participation in historical documentation.

Furthermore, the legal frameworks that allowed sundown towns to exist are crucial to understanding their historical context. Archiving legal documents, such as ordinances, enforcement records, and court cases, provides insight into the systemic nature of racial discrimination in the United States. These records can reveal how laws were used to maintain segregation and provide a foundation for understanding the evolution of civil rights legislation. Analyzing these legal frameworks within the context of archival research can illuminate the failures and successes of various movements aimed at dismantling systemic racism, offering lessons for contemporary advocacy.

Ultimately, the archiving of historical records related to sundown towns is an act of remembrance and a call to action. By preserving these stories and documents, we acknowledge the pain of the past while promoting awareness and education about the ongoing effects of racial segregation. This work is not merely about cataloging history; it is about fostering a critical understanding of the present and encouraging dialogue about racial equity and justice. As we move towards a future that acknowledges the complexities of our past, the archives serve as both a testament to the resilience of marginalized communities and a guide for building a more inclusive society.

The Importance of Oral Histories

The importance of oral histories in understanding sundown towns cannot be overstated. These narratives serve as vital records of individual experiences, illuminating the often-hidden truths about the racial dynamics that shaped these communities. Oral histories provide context that traditional historical records might overlook, allowing for a more nuanced understanding of the societal structures that enforced segregation. Through personal testimonies, we gain insight into the lived experiences of those impacted by sundown town policies, revealing the emotional and psychological scars left by systemic racism.

Oral histories also bridge the gap between generations, enabling descendants of sundown town residents to connect with their family's past. For individuals who may not have access to formal historical accounts, these narratives can be a crucial link to understanding their heritage and the broader implications of their community's history. They highlight the resilience of those who lived within these oppressive environments, showcasing stories of resistance, survival, and the fight for dignity. By documenting these oral histories, we preserve the voices of those who might otherwise be forgotten, ensuring that their experiences contribute to the ongoing dialogue about race and identity in America.

Moreover, oral histories are instrumental in fostering a sense of community and collective memory. In the context of sundown towns, where exclusion and intimidation were prevalent, sharing personal stories can serve as a form of catharsis. It allows individuals to process their experiences and acknowledge the pain inflicted by these communities. This communal storytelling can also promote healing, as it encourages discussions about the past that may have been silenced or ignored. By bringing these narratives to the forefront, we can create a more inclusive understanding of history that recognizes the complexity of human experiences in the context of racial injustice.

The role of oral histories extends beyond individual and communal healing; they also serve as essential tools for education. In academic settings, these narratives can enrich discussions about systemic racism, historical context, and the sociological impacts of sundown towns. They provide real-life examples that challenge students to engage critically with the material, fostering a deeper understanding of the consequences of exclusionary practices. Incorporating oral histories into educational programs can help dismantle the myths surrounding sundown towns, promoting awareness and encouraging discussions about modern racial dynamics.

Finally, the preservation of oral histories is crucial for future generations. As communities continue to grapple with the legacy of sundown towns, these narratives offer invaluable insights into how past injustices shape present realities. By documenting and archiving these stories, we ensure that the lessons learned from the experiences of those who lived in sundown towns remain accessible. This preservation is not just about remembering the past; it is about informing the future, guiding efforts to address ongoing racial inequalities and fostering a more equitable society.

Efforts in Preservation

Efforts in preservation regarding sundown towns have gained momentum as communities confront their historical legacies and seek to rectify the injustices of the past. Preservation initiatives often focus on documenting the history of these towns, ensuring that the narratives of those affected by the discriminatory practices are not forgotten. Local historical societies, museums, and academic institutions are increasingly collaborating to create comprehensive archives that include personal stories, legal documents, and photographs. These resources serve as crucial tools for educating the public about the realities of sundown towns and the broader context of racial segregation in America.

One significant aspect of preservation involves the establishment of educational programs aimed at raising awareness about the legacy of sundown towns. Schools and community organizations are developing curricula that address the historical and sociological impacts of these towns on both local and national levels. By incorporating this history into educational settings, younger generations can gain a deeper understanding of racial dynamics and the ongoing consequences of segregation. This proactive approach not only honors the experiences of those who suffered under these oppressive systems but also fosters dialogue about contemporary issues of race and equality.

In addition to educational initiatives, public art projects and memorials are emerging as powerful tools for remembering the communities affected by sundown practices. Artists and activists are collaborating to create installations that reflect the stories of those who were expelled or marginalized. These projects aim to evoke empathy and provoke thought, encouraging community members to engage with their town's history. Such artistic expressions can serve as focal points for discussions on racial justice and reconciliation, making the past relevant to current social movements.

Local governments and advocacy groups are also advocating for policy changes that recognize and address the legacies of sundown towns. Efforts include land acknowledgments, reparations initiatives, and community reinvestment programs aimed at healing historical wounds. By acknowledging the impact of past injustices, these movements seek to create a more inclusive environment for all residents. This legal and political engagement is crucial for ensuring that the lessons learned from the history of sundown towns inform contemporary policies and practices aimed at fostering racial equity.

Ultimately, the preservation of sundown town histories is not just about remembering the past; it is about shaping a more just future. By actively engaging with the legacies of these communities, individuals and organizations can work together to dismantle the structural racism that persists today. Through education, memorialization, and policy reform, society can honor the resilience of those who fought against oppression and strive toward a future where all individuals are valued and included, regardless of their racial or ethnic background.

Chapter 10: Educational Programs Addressing the Legacy of Sundown Towns

Curriculum Development and Inclusion

Curriculum development in the context of sundown towns requires a comprehensive approach that integrates historical, social, and legal perspectives to foster a more inclusive understanding of America's racial dynamics. In the years leading to 2030, educational institutions must prioritize the creation of curricula that not only address the existence of sundown towns but also highlight their lasting impacts on contemporary society. This development involves collaborating with historians, sociologists, and community leaders to ensure that educational materials reflect the complexities of racial segregation and its ramifications on both individuals and communities.

Inclusion in curriculum development means actively engaging with the narratives of those who were marginalized by sundown town policies. It is essential to incorporate personal stories from descendants of those who lived in these towns, as these accounts provide vital insights into the emotional and psychological toll of systemic racism. Such narratives can serve as powerful teaching tools, allowing students to empathize with the experiences of others and understand the continuity of racial issues in modern America. By giving voice to these histories, educational programs can promote a more nuanced understanding of the past.

Moreover, addressing the legal frameworks surrounding sundown towns is crucial for a well-rounded educational approach. Students should learn about the laws and policies that facilitated racial exclusion, as well as the subsequent legal battles aimed at dismantling such structures. Understanding the historical context of these laws provides a foundation for discussions about current legal issues related to race and discrimination. This knowledge empowers students to critically analyze contemporary legislation and its implications for racial justice, encouraging them to become informed advocates for change.

Incorporating sociological impacts into the curriculum can enhance students' understanding of how sundown towns shaped community development and dynamics. This aspect of the curriculum should focus on the long-term effects of exclusionary practices, including economic disparities and social fragmentation that persist in many communities today. By examining case studies of sundown towns, students can explore patterns of segregation and resilience, drawing connections between historical injustices and present-day challenges. Such analysis fosters a critical awareness of how communities can both perpetuate and combat systemic inequities.

Finally, educational programs must emphasize the importance of documentation and preservation of sundown town histories. This can involve collaborative projects between students and local historians or community organizations to archive oral histories, photographs, and documents related to sundown towns. Engaging students in this process not only enriches their learning experience but also contributes to the broader goal of acknowledging and addressing the legacy of racial exclusion in America. By prioritizing curriculum development that embodies these principles, educators can cultivate a more inclusive and informed citizenry prepared to confront the shadows of the past and advocate for a more equitable future.

Community Outreach and Engagement

Community outreach and engagement are crucial components in addressing the legacy of sundown towns and their modern implications. As communities grapple with their histories, it is essential to create spaces for dialogue that acknowledge the past while fostering a sense of belonging for all residents. Effective outreach initiatives can bridge divides, encouraging residents to confront uncomfortable truths about their town's history and to engage in meaningful discussions about inclusivity. By understanding the dynamics of sundown towns, communities can begin to dismantle the remnants of segregation that persist into the present, paving the way for a more equitable future.

Educational programs play a pivotal role in community outreach efforts. Schools and local organizations can implement curricula that explore the history of sundown towns, focusing on the mechanisms of exclusion and their lasting impacts on racial dynamics. These programs can facilitate workshops, discussions, and presentations that not only educate but also empower community members to reflect on their town's legacy. By engaging students and adults alike, communities can cultivate awareness and foster critical thinking about race, identity, and belonging, which are essential for creating an inclusive environment.

Collaborative projects that involve individuals from diverse backgrounds can further enhance community engagement. Initiatives such as storytelling events, art installations, and public forums can provide platforms for marginalized voices to be heard and recognized. These projects can highlight personal narratives from descendants of sundown town residents, offering insights into the lived experiences shaped by systemic racism. By amplifying these stories, communities can honor their histories while promoting empathy and understanding among residents, thus strengthening social cohesion.

In addition to educational and collaborative efforts, partnerships with local government and law enforcement can help address the lingering effects of sundown town policies. By involving these institutions in outreach initiatives, communities can promote transparency and accountability. Law enforcement agencies can participate in dialogue sessions to address past injustices and work towards rebuilding trust within the community. This engagement can lead to the development of policies that ensure safety and equality for all residents, reinforcing the notion that every individual has a rightful place in the community, regardless of their background.

Ultimately, community outreach and engagement are essential for confronting the legacy of sundown towns in modern America. Through education, collaboration, and institutional involvement, communities can foster an environment where all residents feel valued and included. By actively engaging with their past and working together towards a more equitable future, towns can transform their narratives from exclusion to inclusion, ensuring that the shadows of the past do not dictate the course of their future.

Case Studies of Successful Programs

Case studies of successful programs addressing the legacy of sundown towns provide valuable insights into how communities can confront their past and foster inclusivity. One notable example is the initiative launched in the town of Anna, Illinois, which was historically a sundown town. In response to its racially exclusionary history, local leaders established the Anna Cultural and Historical Commission. This commission aimed to educate residents about the town's past while promoting diversity through community events celebrating different cultures. By incorporating educational workshops and local history projects, the program successfully engaged residents in dialogues about race and reconciliation.

Another significant case study can be found in the town of McKeesport, Pennsylvania. After recognizing its sundown town legacy, community organizers partnered with local schools and universities to implement a comprehensive curriculum focused on racial history and social justice. This educational initiative not only addressed historical injustices but also encouraged students to participate in community service projects that support marginalized groups. Through these efforts, the program aimed to redefine community identity and foster a sense of belonging for all residents, regardless of race.

In the Midwest, the town of Highland Park, Michigan, developed a unique approach to healing the wounds of its past. The community launched a series of storytelling events where descendants of past residents shared their experiences related to the town's history of racial exclusion. These narratives were woven into a broader community dialogue, allowing for collective reflection and healing. The storytelling approach fostered empathy and understanding among residents and helped create a more inclusive environment, encouraging participation from all demographic groups.

A further example is found in the state of California, where a coalition of activists in the former sundown town of Cloverdale initiated a series of public art projects. These projects not only highlighted the history of racial exclusion but also celebrated the contributions of diverse communities to the town's culture. The art installations served as powerful reminders of the need for inclusivity and respect, while also transforming public spaces into venues for community engagement and dialogue. This creative approach not only beautified the town but also sparked conversations about race and community identity.

Lastly, the town of Belvidere, Illinois, has implemented a community policing program aimed at rebuilding trust between law enforcement and marginalized groups. Recognizing the historical role of law enforcement in enforcing sundown policies, local police initiated outreach programs that prioritize relationship-building with diverse populations. By hosting community forums and participating in cultural events, the police department has worked to change perceptions and foster a safer, more inclusive environment. This proactive approach highlights the importance of addressing historical grievances while moving towards a future that embraces diversity and unity.

Chapter 11: Comparative Studies of Sundown

Towns in Different Regions

Regional Variations in Sundown Towns

Regional variations in sundown towns reveal a complex tapestry of racial segregation strategies employed across different parts of the United States. The characteristics and enforcement of sundown town policies varied significantly based on geographic, cultural, and historical contexts. In the Midwest, for example, sundown towns often utilized formal ordinances and community meetings to establish their racial exclusion. Towns like Robinson, Illinois, had signage at their borders warning Black individuals to vacate by sunset. This public declaration of racial boundaries was a method of both intimidation and social control, reflecting the region's historical reliance on agriculture and a predominantly white labor force.

In contrast, the Deep South exhibited more overtly violent means of enforcement. The legacy of slavery and the subsequent Jim Crow laws created an environment where sundown practices were often maintained through brutal means. In towns such as Forsyth County, Georgia, the history is marked by lynchings and violent expulsions, reinforcing a culture of fear that kept Black residents from returning after dark.

This stark difference in the enforcement of sundown town policies illustrates how local histories and legacies of racism shaped the experiences of Black individuals across the nation.

The West also presents a unique case with its own set of sundown towns, often influenced by the migration patterns of the early 20th century. In communities like Lodi, California, the exclusionary practices were less about formal laws and more about social norms and the tacit agreement among residents to maintain racial homogeneity. Here, the absence of explicit signage did not diminish the impact of the unwritten rules that dictated who could reside in or visit the town after dark. The subtleties of these practices highlight the adaptability of sundown town policies to different regional contexts while maintaining their core objective of racial exclusion.

The urban-rural divide further complicates the understanding of sundown towns. In some urban areas, sundown practices were less prevalent due to the higher population density and diverse demographics. However, surrounding suburbs often adopted sundown policies to preserve perceived community values and whiteness. This suburbanization of racism illustrates how sundown town legacies have not only persisted but have also evolved, affecting modern racial dynamics and the makeup of communities in ways that are often overlooked.

Finally, contemporary reflections on sundown towns reveal that their legacies are not confined to the past. Many regions still bear the scars of these discriminatory practices, affecting everything from housing policies to social interactions among different racial groups. Understanding the regional variations in sundown towns allows for a deeper comprehension of the systemic racism that continues to influence American society. By exploring these differences, we can better appreciate the historical context and the ongoing impact of sundown towns on modern racial dynamics.

Comparative Analysis of Racial Dynamics

The legacy of sundown towns in modern America reveals a complex interplay of racial dynamics that continues to shape communities today. Sundown towns were often characterized by explicit and implicit policies that enforced a racially homogeneous environment. This exclusionary practice was sustained through both social norms and legal frameworks designed to maintain white dominance. As we examine the historical context of these towns, it becomes clear that their impact extends far beyond the past, influencing contemporary racial relations and community structures.

Comparative analysis of racial dynamics across different regions in the United States highlights significant variations in how sundown towns have evolved and how their legacies have been navigated. In some areas, the remnants of these towns are evident in persistent racial segregation and economic disparities. Conversely, other regions have seen efforts toward reconciliation and integration. Understanding these differences is crucial for grasping how historical injustices continue to manifest in present-day communities, creating a patchwork of racial experiences across the nation.

The enforcement of sundown policies often relied on local law enforcement, which played a critical role in upholding the racial order. In many towns, police were either complicit or actively involved in acts of intimidation against Black individuals. This relationship between law enforcement and racial exclusion set a precedent for ongoing distrust in communities that have a history of racial violence. In analyzing these dynamics, it becomes evident that the legacy of law enforcement practices during the sundown era continues to affect interactions between police and marginalized communities today.

Additionally, personal narratives from the descendants of sundown town residents provide valuable insights into the lasting emotional and psychological impacts of these historical practices. Many descendants of those who enforced sundown policies grapple with the shame and guilt associated with their family's past actions. These stories illustrate the complexity of inherited legacies and the ongoing struggle for understanding and atonement within families and communities. They also highlight the need for educational programs that address these histories and foster dialogue about race and inclusion.

The sociological implications of sundown towns extend into community development, shaping economic opportunities and social relationships. Areas that were once sundown towns often struggle with economic stagnation and demographic challenges. By examining these towns in a comparative framework, it becomes apparent that the historical exclusion of Black individuals has left deep scars that affect not only the economic viability of these communities but also the social fabric that binds residents together. Acknowledging and addressing these dynamics is essential for fostering healing and promoting equitable development in the years to come.

Lessons from Diverse Experiences

The legacy of sundown towns in America offers crucial lessons borne from the complexities of racial dynamics and community development. These towns, through a combination of discriminatory laws and societal norms, systematically marginalized Black individuals, enforcing a racial hierarchy that persisted well into modern times. The characteristics of sundown towns—where Black individuals could only enter during daylight hours and faced violence if they remained after dark—illustrate a stark reality of exclusion. Understanding these conditions helps illuminate the broader socio-political landscape that has shaped contemporary racial relations across the nation.

Analyzing the historical context of sundown towns reveals the mechanisms through which systemic racism was institutionalized. The social fabric of these communities was woven with fear and exclusion, as local laws and community practices reinforced a sense of entitlement among white residents. Personal narratives from descendants of both Black individuals who faced expulsion and white residents who lived in these towns provide valuable insights into the emotional and psychological impacts of such a legacy. These stories humanize the statistics, showcasing how the reverberations of past injustices continue to influence present-day attitudes and interactions.

The impact of sundown towns extends beyond historical memory; it permeates modern racial dynamics, often manifesting in implicit biases and ongoing segregation. Communities that once thrived on exclusionary practices now grapple with the consequences of their past, including economic disparities and social fragmentation. The lessons learned from these experiences emphasize the importance of addressing historical injustices to foster healing and reconciliation. Acknowledging the past enables communities to confront lingering prejudices and work toward creating inclusive environments.

Legal frameworks surrounding sundown towns highlight the critical role of government in both perpetuating and dismantling racial barriers. Many of the laws that enabled these towns to thrive were enacted at local and state levels, demonstrating the power dynamics that existed within governmental structures. Current efforts to rectify these injustices often call for policy reforms and community engagement, stressing the need for a legal reckoning that acknowledges historical wrongs. Understanding these legal implications is essential for advocates working to dismantle systemic racism in contemporary society.

Sundown Towns in American History: Legacy and Modern Impacts The term "sundown towns" historically referred to communities in the United States that systematically excluded nonwhite individuals, particularly African Americans, through formal laws, policies, or informal social practices. These communities enforced restrictions that prohibited people of color from being present within town limits after sundown, often under threat of violence or other forms of intimidation. This practice was most prevalent during the late 19th and early 20th centuries, particularly in regions such as the Midwest, West, and parts of the South. Historical Context Sundown towns emerged during an era of widespread racial segregation and discrimination in the United States. These towns employed various means to enforce exclusion, including: Explicit Ordinances: Local laws explicitly barring African Americans or other nonwhite individuals from residing or being present in the town after dark. Unwritten Rules: Social norms reinforced by threats, intimidation, and violence, often with the tacit approval of local authorities. Signage: Many towns displayed signs at their borders with warnings such as "Don't let the sun set on you here." The rationale for these policies varied but often included maintaining racial purity, preserving property values, or catering to racist sentiments within the white community. Decline of Sundown Town Practices The Civil Rights Movement of the 1950s and 1960s, coupled with federal and state legislation such as the Civil Rights Act of 1964, played a significant role in dismantling overtly discriminatory laws and practices.

Signage and explicit ordinances became illegal, leading to the formal dissolution of sundown town policies.

Lingering Legacies Despite the legal abolition of sundown towns, their legacy continues to influence social and demographic patterns in modern America: Demographic Homogeneity: Many former sundown towns remain predominantly white due to historical exclusionary practices and ongoing implicit biases. Economic Barriers: Economic factors, such as disparities in housing affordability and access to resources, perpetuate segregation in certain communities. Cultural Residues: The social attitudes and perceptions fostered during the sundown town era can persist, subtly influencing interactions and policies. Modern Relevance While explicit enforcement has ended, understanding the historical context of sundown towns is essential to addressing the structural inequalities that remain today. For instance, historian James W. Loewen's research highlights towns like Hawthorne and Taft in California, which were identified as sundown towns. Such examples underscore the need for continuous examination of how historical exclusion shapes present-day demographics and community dynamics. Resources for Further Exploration For those interested in exploring the history and legacy of sundown towns in greater detail, the following resources are recommended: "Sundown Towns: A Hidden Dimension of American Racism" by James W. Loewen – A comprehensive book exploring the history and impact of sundown towns. History and Social Justice Project – This online resource provides a database of known and suspected sundown towns by state, offering valuable insights into their prevalence and characteristics.

Conclusion Understanding sundown towns and their legacy is critical in confronting and addressing the enduring impacts of racial exclusion in the United States. By acknowledging this history, communities can work toward fostering inclusivity and equity, ensuring that the mistakes of the past do not dictate the future.

Title: Shadows at Sundown:
The History and **Legacy of Sundown Towns in America**

Table of Contents:

1. **Introduction**

- Understanding Sundown Towns

- Purpose and Scope of the Book

2. **Chapter 1: The Origins of Sundown Towns**

- Historical Context: Racial Segregation in America

- The Rise of Jim Crow Laws

- The Concept of "Sundown Towns"

3. **Chapter 2: The Mechanisms of Exclusion**

- Legal Framework: Zoning Laws and Ordinances

- The Role of Vigilante Groups

- Community Enforcement: Social Norms and Peer Pressure

4. **Chapter 3: Geographic Distribution of Sundown Towns**

- Mapping Sundown Towns Across the United States

- Case Studies: Notable Sundown Towns and Their Histories

- The Relationship Between Industrialization and Sundown Towns

5. **Chapter 4: Personal Narratives and Oral Histories**

- Testimonies from Former Residents

- The Experiences of African Americans and Other Minorities

- Stories of Resistance and Resilience

6. **Chapter 5: The Impact on Communities**

- Economic Consequences for Excluded Groups

- The Psychological Toll of Living in Sundown Towns

- Long-Term Effects on Racial Relations

11. **Appendices**

- **A. Resources for Further Reading**

- **B. Organizations Working on Racial Justice**

- C. Maps and Data on Sundown Towns

Introduction

As dusk falls, shadows lengthen and the complexities of human history often come to light. In the United States, one of the more insidious aspects of this history lies in the phenomenon known as "sundown towns"—communities that enforced racial exclusion after dark. This book seeks to explore the origins, mechanisms, and lasting impacts of sundown towns, shedding light on a chapter of American history that continues to resonate in contemporary society.

Chapter 1: The Origins of Sundown Towns

The story of sundown towns is intricately tied to the broader narrative of racial segregation in America. Emerging in the late 19th century, these towns implemented unwritten or explicit rules that forbade people of color from being present after sunset. This chapter will delve into the socio-political conditions that gave rise to these towns and the societal attitudes that allowed such practices to flourish.

Chapter 2: The Mechanisms of Exclusion

Sundown towns employed a variety of strategies to enforce segregation, from discriminatory zoning laws to the intimidation tactics of local vigilante groups. This chapter will analyze these mechanisms and the role of community complicity in maintaining an atmosphere of exclusion.

Chapter 3: Geographic Distribution of Sundown Towns

Sundown towns were not confined to any one region; they appeared across the United States. This chapter will provide a geographic overview, highlighting key case studies that illustrate the prevalence of these towns and their unique histories.

Chapter 4: Personal Narratives and Oral Histories

The stories of those who lived in or were affected by sundown towns add a deeply human element to this historical account. This chapter will feature personal narratives, highlighting the resilience, fear, and courage of individuals who navigated these challenging environments.

Chapter 5: The Impact on Communities

The existence of sundown towns had profound economic and psychological impacts, not only on the excluded populations but also on the communities themselves. This chapter will explore these effects and their implications for understanding racial dynamics in America.

Chapter 6: The Civil Rights Movement and Sundown Towns

As the Civil Rights Movement gained momentum, sundown towns became focal points for activists seeking to dismantle systemic racism. This chapter will examine key events and strategies employed in the struggle against these towns and the barriers that still existed.

Chapter 7: Sundown Towns in Contemporary America

While many sundown towns have changed, their legacy endures. This chapter will analyze how contemporary communities grapple with this history and

The trickery of AI technology lets you talk to Jesus or Satan.

Jim Crow still exist in America 2025 - 2030

Don't be caught in a sun downtown after the Sunset

Jim Crow Courthouse theater America

Jim Crow Deep State

2030

The holy church of Jim Crow

AI-generated image of Vatican 'devil worship' goes viral

It's a take over not a make over

AI New World religion

The rise of artificial intelligence (AI) could lead to the emergence of new religions

The Touch of Class

Agent's of Satan

The rise of artificial intelligence (AI) could lead to the emergence of new religions.

71

Made in United States
Cleveland, OH
26 March 2025

15534891R00042